What on Earth Books is an imprint of What on Earth Publishing
The Black Barn, Wickhurst Farm, Tonbridge, Kent TN11 8PS, United Kingdom
30 Ridge Road Unit B, Greenbelt, Maryland, 20770, United States

First published in English in 2020 by What on Earth Books

First published in France under the title *Chaque seconde dans le monde* © Actes Sud, Paris, 2018

Text and illustrations by Bruno Gibert
Translation © What on Earth Publishing, 2020

Staff for this edition:
Translation and editing: Patrick Skipworth
Cover design: Daisy Symes and Andy Forshaw
Fact-checking: Michelle Harris

Library of Congress Cataloging-in-Publication Data available upon request

ISBN: 978-1-912920-30-3

Printed in India

10 9 8 7 6 5 4 3 2 1

EVERY SECOND

BY
**BRUNO
GIBERT**

Every second, around the world

wedding is celebrated,

4

babies are born,

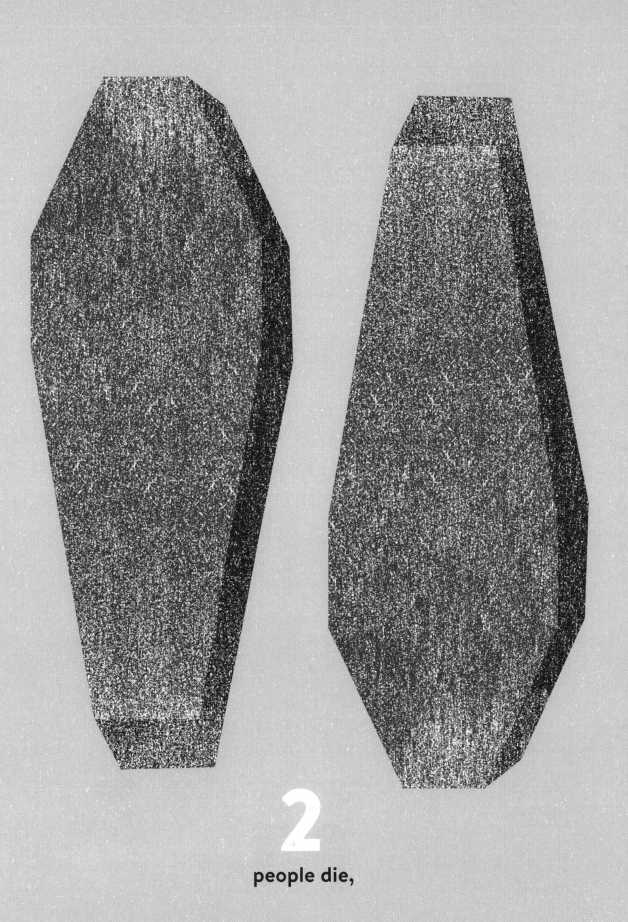

2
people die,

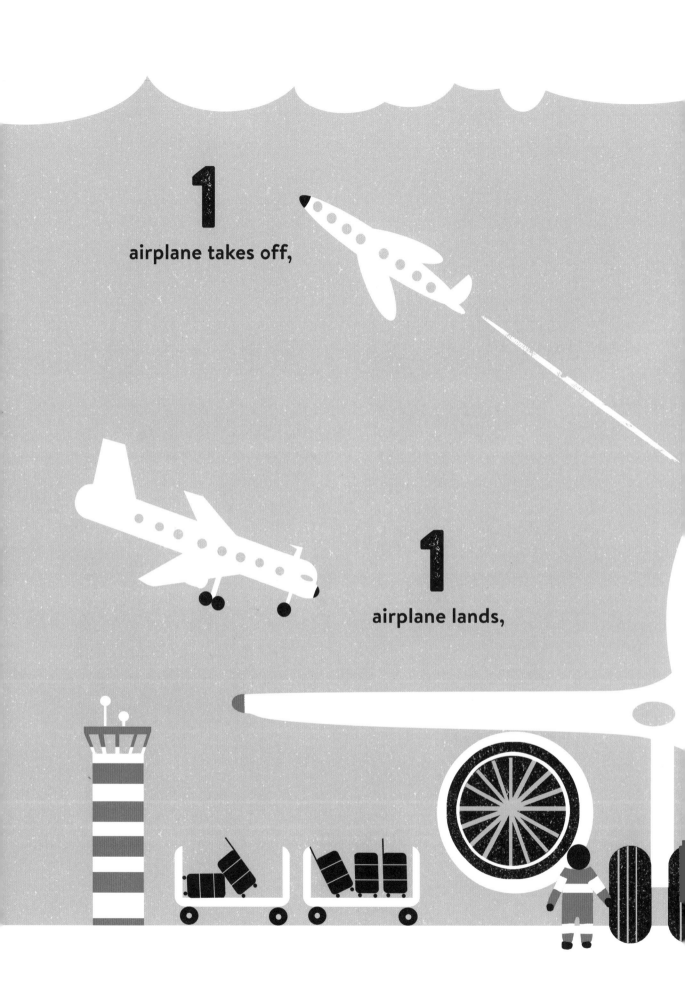

1

airplane takes off,

1

airplane lands,

130

air passengers climb aboard,

200,000

text messages are sent,

and

3,000,000

emails,

73,000

pounds of goods are
traveling across the sea,
(330,000 kilograms)

2,300

packages are shipped,

40
pairs of jeans

and

500

pairs of shoes are sold,

48

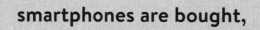

smartphones are bought,

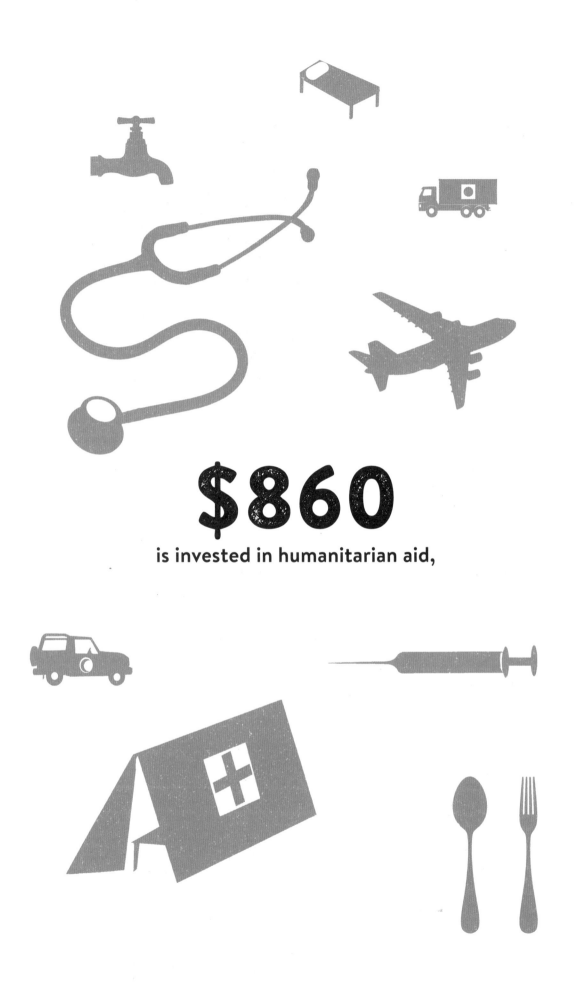

$860

is invested in humanitarian aid,

$57,700

is spent on arms and weapons,

3,300

pounds of beef are devoured,
(1,500 kilograms)

8,000

scoops of ice cream are eaten,

That's 430 quarts (410 liters).

6,700

drink cans are opened,

12,100

pounds of sugar are consumed,
(5,500 kilograms)

220

pounds of cocoa
are made into chocolate,
(100 kilograms)

2,050

chicks hatch from their eggs,

7,400 quarts of milk are taken from cows,
(7,000 liters)

1,050,000

gallons of gas are produced by cows
(from both ends),
(3,000,000 liters)

20,300

pounds of poop
are made by humans,
(9,200 kilograms)

23,300

pounds of household
waste are produced,
(10,600 kilograms)

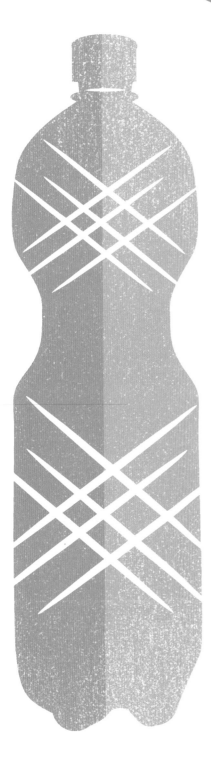

20,000

plastic bottles are produced,

but only

1,600

of them are recycled,

38

tires are made,

370,000

miles are traveled by car,
(600,000 kilometers)

That's more than the distance between the Earth and the Moon.

2
car accidents
lead to injuries,

100

lightning bolts
strike the Earth,

4,500

Olympic-sized swimming pools of water evaporate from the oceans,

An Olympic-sized swimming pool holds 800,000 gallons (3,000,000 liters) of water.

11,500

pounds of sand, carried by
the wind, leave the Sahara desert,
(5,235 kilograms)

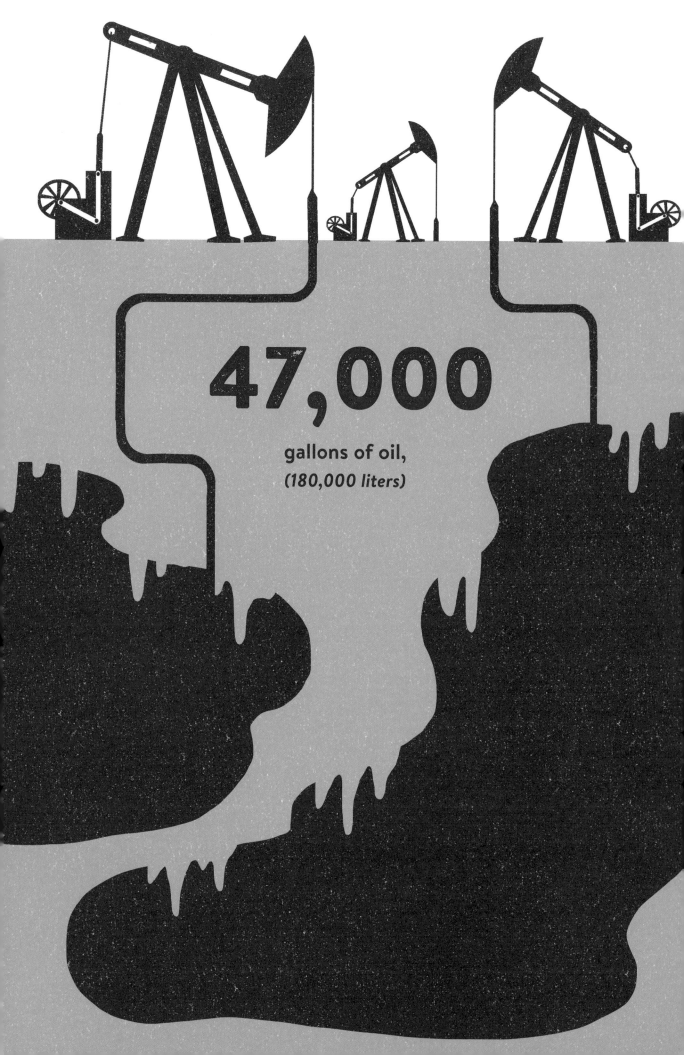

47,000

gallons of oil,
(180,000 liters)

and

0.32

ounces of gold *(9 grams)*
are extracted from below
the Earth's surface,

485

trees are cut down

and

158

are replanted,

3.3

**pounds of meteorites
fall from the sky,**
(1.5 kilograms)

and the Earth travels miles around the Sun.
(30 kilometers)

Every second,
every minute,
ever hour,
every day,
every year,
so many things happen
around the world.

SOURCES

"World Marriage Data," United Nations Department of Economic and Social Affairs (https://www.un.org/en/development/desa/population/publications/dataset/marriage/data.asp)

"2018 World Population Data Sheet," Population Reference Bureau (https://www.prb.org/wp-content/uploads/2018/08/2018_WPDS.pdf)

"Industry Statistics Fact Sheet," IATA (https://www.iata.org/pressroom/facts_figures/fact_sheets/Documents/fact-sheet-industry-facts.pdf)

"Daily SMS Mobile Usage Statistics," SMSEagle (https://www.smseagle.eu/2017/03/06/daily-sms-mobile-statistics/)

"Number of sent and received e-mails per day worldwide from 2017 to 2023 (in billions)," Statista (https://www.statista.com/statistics/456500/daily-number-of-e-mails-worldwide/)

"Email Statistics Report, 2015–2019," Radicati (https://www.radicati.com/wp/wp-content/uploads/2015/02/Email-Statistics-Report-2015-2019-Executive-Summary.pdf)

"Review of Maritime Transport 2018," United Nations Conference on Trade and Development (https://unctad.org/en/PublicationsLibrary/rmt2018_en.pdf)

"Global shipping volumes hit new high and set to surpass 100 billion by 2020," eDelivery (https://edelivery.net/2018/08/parcel-shipping-volumes-hit/)

"Denim Jeans Industry Market Analysis," Statistic Brain Research Institute (https://www.statisticbrain.com/denim-jeans-industry-statistics/)

"The Size of the Global Footwear Market," Common Objective (https://www.commonobjective.co/article/the-size-of-the-global-footwear-market)

"Number of smartphones sold to end users worldwide from 2007 to 2020 (in million units)," Statista (https://www.statista.com/statistics/263437/global-smartphone-sales-to-end-users-since-2007/)

"Global humanitarian assistance report 2018," Development Initiatives (http://devinit.org/wp-content/uploads/2018/06/GHA-Report-2018.pdf)

"Trends in World Military Expenditure," 2018, SIPRI, https://www.sipri.org/sites/default/files/2019-04/fs_1904_milex_2018.pdf

"Meat consumption," OECD Data (https://data.oecd.org/agroutput/meat-consumption.htm)

"Ice Cream: Global Intelligence Database," Research and Markets (https://www.researchandmarkets.com/research/g5dq8w/global_ice_cream?w=5)

"Aluminium cans (production and consumption data)," The World Counts (https://www.theworldcounts.com/counters/world_food_consumption_statistics/aluminium_cans_facts)

"Cocoa Market Update," World Cocoa Foundation (http://www.worldcocoafoundation.org/wp-content/uploads/Cocoa-Market-Update-as-of-4-1-2014.pdf)

Gorman, James. "It Could Be the Age of the Chicken, Geologically," *The New York Times* (https://www.nytimes.com/2018/12/11/science/chicken-anthropocene-archaeology.html)

"Global milk consumption in 2013 and 2016 (in billion liters)," Statista (https://www.statista.com/statistics/263955/consumption-of-milk-worldwide-since-2001/)

Silverman, Jacob. "Do cows pollute as much as cars?," *How Stuff Works* (https://animals.howstuffworks.com/mammals/methane-cow.htm)

Kluger, Jeffrey. "How poop can be worth $9.5 billion," *Time* (https://time.com/4098127/human-waste-energy-recycling/)

"Trends in Sold Waste Management," The World Bank (http://datatopics.worldbank.org/what-a-waste/trends_in_solid_waste_management.html)

Laville, Sandra and Taylor, Matthew. "A million bottles a minute: world's plastic binge 'as dangerous as climate change," *The Guardian* (https://www.theguardian.com/environment/2017/jun/28/a-million-a-minute-worlds-plastic-bottle-binge-as-dangerous-as-climate-change)

"2018 production statistics," OICA (http://www.oica.net/category/production-statistics/2018-statistics/)

"Projected worldwide tire market volume from 2014 to 2018 (in billion units)," Statista (https://www.statista.com/statistics/625275/global-tire-market-volume/)

"Road safety facts," ASIRT (https://www.asirt.org/safe-travel/road-safety-facts/)

"Lightning," *National Geographic* (https://www.nationalgeographic.com/environment/natural-disasters/lightning/)

"The Water Cycle - A Climate Change Perspective," Windows to the Universe, (https://www.windows2universe.org/earth/Water/water_cycle_climate_change.html)

"Desert Dust Feeds Amazon Forests," NASA (https://science.nasa.gov/science-news/science-at-nasa/2015/29apr_amazondust)

"Oil Statistics," IEA (https://www.iea.org/statistics/oil/)

"How much gold has been mined?," World Gold Council (https://www.gold.org/about-gold/gold-supply/gold-mining/how-much-gold)

Startin, Adam. "Fact check: are there really more trees today than 100 years ago?," tentree (https://www.tentree.com/blogs/posts/fact-check-are-there-really-more-trees-today-than-100-years-ago)

Crowther, T. W. et al. "Mapping tree density at a global scale," *Nature* 525, 201–205 (10 September 2015)

"How giant meteorites hit Earth each year," Ask an Astronomer (http://curious.astro.cornell.edu/our-solar-system/75-our-solar-system/comets-meteors-and-asteroids/meteorites/313-how-many-meteorites-hit-earth-each-year-intermediate)

"At what speed does the Earth move around the Sun?," Ask an Astronomer (http://curious.astro.cornell.edu/about-us/41-our-solar-system/the-earth/orbit/91-at-what-speed-does-the-earth-move-around-the-sun-beginner)